DON GOSSETT

Gladness

THE KEY

TO

ANOINTED LIVING

"God has anointed you with the oil of gladness"
Hebrews 1:9

Gladness: The Key to Anointed Living
Don Gossett
Box 2
Blaine, Washington 98230

©Copyright 1991 by Don Gossett
Printed in the United States of America

INTRODUCTION

Gladness: The Key to Anionted Living

"Your God has anointed you with the oil of gladness"
Hebrews 1:9

"The yoke will be destroyed because of the anionting oil"
Isaiah 10:27

As you study this book and act upon its teachings, may you experience the fresh oil anointing of gladness in high degree.

ETERNALLY GRATEFUL TO JESUS

What a sacred thing is the presence of the Holy Spirit upon a life! I became aware of this presence when I was a small boy. The Holy Spirit began His precious, deep inner working when I knew very little about the Bible or the real plan of salvation.

There were many steps before I came to receive Jesus Christ .... the times I heard my Uncle Jimmie Rogers preach, and then would go home and try to imitate him .... the time when my dad gave consent for Christians to build an old-fashioned brush arbor on my dad's farm, and I would stand outside those brush arbor meetings and listen to the preaching, and behold the wonder of sinners going forward to accept Christ ... the times when my Sunday School teachers talked with me tenderly about the Lord... these were stepping stones to that decision I made one Sunday night in 1941, when I was barely 12 years of age.

Why did I wait until I was twelve? Somehow, I had the idea, passed along to me by others, that it didn't matter whether one was saved or not, before the age of 12, that you would still go to heaven. It was this unfounded concept that if you die before age 12, one goes to heaven anyway. Ridiculous, I know, but like many others, I believed it.

I knew that salvation was based upon what Jesus Christ did for us, in taking our place on the cross, to suffer the penalty for all our sins.

In that great old Baptist church I went with some neighbors for the final service of a "revival meeting." The evangelist portrayed Christ dying on the cross with real drama. But the truth of it penetrated my boyish heart.

When the invitation was given and the congregation was singing, "Softly and Tenderly Jesus Is Calling," that night I made the "decision of decisions" .... I went forward to accept Jesus Christ as my own personal Saviour.

While I didn't understand the full impact of what happened that night, I knew I was saved. Going to bed that night was a different experience. I was almost spellbound by the sure knowledge I was now a Christian.

"Glad that I'm a Christian, been washed in the blood, now I am changed!"

The next day at school, a friend named Ralph came up to me at the ball field, and said, "My mother was at that meeting last night; she said you got saved. Did you really?"

"Yes, I did, Ralph," I replied

"Well, how does it feel to be saved?"

"I can't quite describe it. But it sure is wonderful to know that I'm saved."

Ralph looked at me longingly and said, "Boy, it must make you glad to be a Christian."

"Yes, I am very glad that I'm a Christian," I told him, and with those words, off we went for our school ball game.

FULL ASSURANCE OF FAITH

After I received Jesus Christ by faith into my life, there were yet times that I had doubts about my salvation. These doubts were caused by unsaved people who jeered the Bible and things of God. Also, I often pondered if I had the right "feelings" a Christian should have. Then, too, when I would fail the Lord, I wondered if there were anything to my supposedly being saved.

But in my quest, God gave me "the full assurance of faith" (Heb. 10:22), and cured me of all my doubtings. Praise His Name.

How did I attain this full assurance of faith? From God's wonderful Word!

"Nobody can know for sure he is saved." This is what a man told me, whom I once met and shared with him my knowledge of salvation through Christ.

"Never in this life can a person know he is saved," the man continued. "You just must keep on doing the best you can, and when the books are opened you will find out whether you made it or not."

This worried me. I was trying my best to be a Christian. What if this man is right? As a youngster, this really bothered me.

I cannot say the full understanding of my sure relationship with God came instantly. Rather, it was a matter of learning "the truth, and the truth shall set you free," declared Jesus.

Peace With God. I'm glad I'm a Christian because of the peace with God I gained when I accepted Christ by faith. "Therefore being justified by faith, we have peace with God through our Lord Jesus Christ" Rom 5:1. As long as I resisted the call of the Spirit to accept Christ as my Saviour, I was warring against God, I was His enemy, even though He loved me. But then when I ceased resisting and by faith received Him,

4

I had peace with God!

Full Authority To Know. "As many as received Him, to them gave He power to become the sons of God, even to them that believe on His Name" Jn 1:12. I received Christ; therefore I knew I was a son of God, His own child.

This power I received had changed me, transformed me, made me anew. Hallelujah! O the wonder of receiving Christ, then knowing I was saved.

Another great truth that gave me victory over doubts was this one: "The Spirit itself beareth witness with our spirit, that we are the sons of God" Rom 8:16. I received the witness of the Spirit of God, that I belonged to Him. This was precious to know.

Doubts are only cast out by truth. And the truth of God did its work in my heart. "We know that we have passed from death unto life, because we love the brethren" I Jn 3:14. When I was saved, and knew it, I discovered that hates, grudges and unforgiveness towards those who had wronged me were gone. I loved others, especially fellow Christians, but also God enabled me to love those who I, in the natural order of things, didn't like. Thank God for His love that passes understanding.

It is not presumption to declare, here and now in this life, that one is saved. "He that hath the Son hath life" I Jn 5:12. I knew I had received the Son of God into my heart, and I knew His divine life was within me.

"If any man be in Christ, he is a new creature; the old things are passed away; behold, all things are become new" II Cor. 5:17.

God declares this is His Word. I knew I was a new creature in Christ. This was by His grace, through faith in Jesus Christ.

God had said so, and "God is not a man that He should lie" Num. 23:19.

I have deep assurance that one day I will meet Christ face to face. My assurance doesn't rest on feelings alone, but on God's Word. And His Word is like an anchor, it holds me steadfast and sure!

THE JOY-FILLED LIFE

Outside of the Christian life I have found a limited happiness and pleasure. For instance, being an athlete and achieving some honors brought a measure of happiness. Being elected the president of my high school student body was indeed a satisfying experience.

And there have been other facets of life that have brought pleasure.

However, it has been my experience, along with many others, to discover that the life of "Christ within" is the real joy-filled life. I am convinced that JOY is only found in the Christian life. For this joy is something Jesus brought to the earth. The angel sang, "Behold I bring unto you good tidings of great joy, which shall be to all the people, for unto you is born this day .... a Saviour, which is Christ the Lord" Lk. 2. And Jesus gave us joyful words just before He returned to heaven, "These things have I spoken unto you, that my joy may be in you, and your joy shall be full" Jn 15:11.

Yes, it is this joy that makes the Christian's life different from people of the world. "The joy of the Lord is your strength" Neh. 8:10. And this joy holds the Christian steadfast in times of stress. He can rejoice when all others are miserable.

James said, "My brethren, count it all joy when ye fall into divers temptations, knowing this, that the trying of your faith worketh patience" James 1:2,3. Jesus taught, "Blessed are ye, when men shall revile you, and shall say all manner of evil against you falsely, for my sake. Rejoice, and be exceeding glad: for great is your reward in heaven" Matt 5:11-12.

The disciples rejoiced because they were accounted worthy to suffer shame for Christ's name (Acts 5:40). Paul and Silas sang praises to God in the most uncomfortable of circumstances (Acts 16:23-25). Paul could say he was always rejoicing even when sorrowful (2 Cor 6:10). Even in these troublesome times, the Christian finds that the joy of the Lord is with him to sustain him.

"This Calls For A Celebration"

This is a familiar expression. But in Lk 5:29 we read of Levi's (Matthew) planning a celebration, not because of any earthly achievement, but because he was turning his back upon selfish life to follow the Lord Jesus. Read about it, "Jesus ... saw a publican, named Levi, sitting at the receipt of the custom: and he said unto him, Follow me. And he left all, rose up, and followed him. And Levi made him a great feast in his own house: and there was a great company of publicans and of others that sat down with them."

There is no greater occasion for rejoicing than the birth of a person into the kingdom of God. Jesus, in applying the truth of the parable of the Lost Sheep, said there is joy in heaven over one sinner that repents. The converts at Samaria found "great joy" when they received Christ, and the Philippian jailer "rejoiced, believing in God with all his house" (Acts 16). So there is rejoicing on earth, too, when a sinner comes to know Christ as personal Saviour!

Salvation is the start of the joy-filled life. Jesus commanded His disciples to rejoice because their names were written down in heaven (Lk. 10:20). Then we read of Zaccheus, after he had come down from the tree, it says he received Jesus joyfully (Lk 19:6).

Fullness of joy is found only in maintaining a close fellowship life, abiding in the presence of Christ. "In thy presence is fullness of joy" Ps. 16:11.

Liberal Giving Produces Joy

A frequently overlooked caused of joy is generosity. When David knew that his days on earth were numbered, he received an offering for he temple which Solomon was going to build. This liberality was followed by expressions of joy. "Then the people rejoiced, for that they offered willingly, because with perfect heart they offered willingly to the Lord. And David the king also rejoiced with great joy" I Chr 29:9.

Some of our most joyful experiences in the realm of faith are in giving unto the Lord. Once my wife and I gave our last dollar in an offering, with real joy, and then we watched God work a miracle for us that brought continuous joy to our hearts.

After we receive Christ, then the absorbing of God's Word becomes a vital cause of joy. "Thy words were found, and I did eat them, and thy Word was unto me the joy and rejoicing of mine heart" Jer. 15:16.

Losing The Joy

One of the great tragedies is that Christians sometimes lose their joy. Definite acts of sin (compare 2 Samuel 12 and Psalm 51), as well as careless drifting from the Lord, are causes for losing the joy of the Lord.

While losing joy is a great tragedy, there is a great assurance in the Bible fact that it can be found again. After David had prayed. "Wash me thoroughly from mine iniquity, and cleanse me from my sin," he could pray also, "Lord, restore unto me the joy of thy salvation" Ps 51:2,12. And the joy of the Lord was restored to him.

If you are one who has lost the joy of the Lord, go before God in heart-searching. Confess every sin unto Him. Ask Him as did David, "Restore unto me the joy of thy salvation." The Lord will surely do it!

We are living in days when barreness of soul characterizes many. If you have lost that vital life of joy through drifting, make it your prayer, "O Lord, wilt thou not revive us again: that thy people may rejoice in thee?" Closeness of fellowship with Christ restores this joy.

It is very important that we keep joy-filled. By a joy-filled life we can be of greater service to others in addition to the personal profit that is ours. A joy-filled life is the best advertisement for the Gospel!

Someone has said, "When you smile, another smiles, and soon that smile will go a mile, until there are miles and miles of smiles - because you smiled."

The joy-filled life is contagious. And it is very attractive in this world of sorrow, disappointment and heartbreak. Thank God for the joy-filled life!

HOW TO RECEIVE GUIDANCE FROM GOD

"Trust in the Lord with all thine heart, lean not to thine own understanding; in all thy ways acknowledge Him, and He shall direct they paths" Proverbs 3:5-6.

Psalm 119:105. "Thy Word is a lamp unto my feet, and a light unto my path." All guidance must be in harmony with the Word, never apart from it. The Holy Ghost always uses the Word - "Taking the sword of the Spirit, which is the Word of God" Ephesians 6:17. For instance, the Holy Spirit never leads a Christian to marry a non-Christian, for that would be a violation of His Word. "Be ye not unequally yoked with unbelievers" II Corinthians 6:14. The Holy Spirit never leads a true Christian to walk in darkness, never. Jesus said, "I am the Light of the world, he that followeth me shall never walk in darkness" John 8:12.

We should not make guidance complicated. Proverbs 16:9, "A man's heart deviseth his way, but the Lord directeth his steps."

We must submit to His Lordship over our lives. "Trust in the Lord with all thine heart." Confess it. "Jesus is Lord; I trust Him with all my heart."

We must resist the enemy by using the authority of Jesus to silence the voice of the enemy. James 4:7, "Resist the devil, and he will flee from you."

John 10:27, "My sheep hear my voice, and I know them, and they follow me." Because we are His sheep, we can expect to have His guidance.

Allow God to speak the way He chooses. Pray as did Samuel, "Speak, Lord, for thy servant heareth." God may choose to speak by an audible voice (Exodus 3:4-5); or by dreams (Matthew 2:13, 22); or by visions (Isaiah 6:1, Revelation 1:12-17).

One of the most usual ways God gives guidance is revealed in Isaiah 30:21, "And thine ears shall hear a word behind thee saying, this is the way, walk ye in it, when ye turn to the right hand, and when ye turn to the left."

Get your own leading from God. Beware of counterfeit guidance. The Lord may use others to confirm your guidance.

"WHO TOLD YOU TO BLOW THE WHISTLE?"

A True Story of Guidance in China

A story comes out of China telling about a woman who was working in a mining operation. One of her duties was to blow the whistle which alerted the miners that it was time to leave the mine for lunch or for the day. Faithfully she performed her duties as instructed by the Communist leadership.

One day this Christian woman experienced a strong inner urge to blow the whistle a full hour before lunch time. There was a great conflict within. What should she do? Her instructions were to wait for another hour - and yet, she sensed the Holy Spirit's strong urging to do it right now. To disobey orders might lead to loss of work - and possibly other consequences! What should she do?

The decision was made, for the impulse was so strong. Indeed, she felt she would disobey God if she didn't blow the whistle. So a full hour before lunch she blew the whistle and all the workers came out of the mine. When the last one emerged, the mine collapsed.

The news about the mine collapse spread quickly around the area. Communist officials and supervisors of the mine operation came to the accident site. They soon discovered that every worker was accounted for - and every one was safe and sound. The hero of the day was they young woman who had called the workers out from their subterranean passages. An interrogation followed.

"Who told you to blow the whistle?" they asked. And she felt compelled to tell exactly what had happened, how the Holy Spirit had urged her to give the life saving alarm. Workers, families, friends and officials - all realised that Almighty God had intervened and prevented a major mining disaster. And this led to a widespread revival of the Gospel of Jesus Christ in that area.

You, too, can be guided by God! You can hear His voice!

A GRATEFUL CHRISTIAN

In blazing letters here is God's Will accurately defined: "In everything give thanks: for this is the will of God in Christ Jesus concerning you" I Th. 5:18. Above all else, I desire to do the will of God. Hence I am a Thanksgiver: one who gives thanks .... in everything.

Another strong New Testament command: "Be ye thankful" Col. 3:15. "Thankful" means to be full of thanks! This is the attitude of gratitude. Often I lift my voice in giving thanks to God for His bountiful blessings. It's the best habit I can ever form! Also, I practice verbal thanks to others.

Once each day, as long as I live, and have a voice, I shall lift up my voice and sing, "Thank you, Lord, for saving my soul!" I shall give thanks for benefits received, by acknowledging His kindness in words of sincere gratitude.

God has a warning of the consequence of losing the attitude of gratitude: "Because that, when they knew God, they glorified Him not as God, neither were thankful; but became vain in their imaginations, and their foolish heart was darkened" Rom. 1:21. Ingratitude extinguishes the light of God in the heart; it is the mark of a foolish heart.

I am aware that a prominent sign of the last days is this spirit of ingratitude: "In the last days, saith God, perilous times shall come. Men shall be ... unthankful" II Tim. 3:1-2. Those who are unthankful are simply fulfilling Bible prophecy! When Jesus healed the ten lepers, nine of ten were unthankful. The percentage has hardly changed today: Only one of ten who has been recipient of the Lord's blessings is truly thankful! I shall be a part of the "mighty minority" who gives thanks to God! A thanksgiver is a non-conformist.

Col. 2:6-7 declares that when I am truly rooted and built up in Christ, and established in the faith, I will be "abounding therein with thanksgiving," which means "overflowing with thanksgiving." If my life in Christ is solid and my faith effective, I shall indeed "overflow with thanksgiving"!

I now possess the attitude of gratitude. I shall ever "be thankful unto Him and bless His name" Ps. 100:4. I will manifest the attitude of gratitude in my own home, with my own loved ones; also, unto others I shall express thanks. The Attitude of Gratitude is so God-pleasing and works wonders in all my relationships!

GLADNESS: A SECRET TO STRENGTH

Greater than any human pleasure or happiness is the joy of the Lord. Joyful Christians are the best advertisement for Christianity. Joyful Christians have always been a challenge and testimonial to a broken-hearted world.

Happiness is the product of our surroundings. It is the thing that satisfies the senses. The material things that bring one happiness may be taken from him in a moment and he is left desolate.

Joy belongs to the spiritual realm just as happiness belongs to the sense realm. When a Christian is not joyful it is either because of broken fellowship or a lack of knowledge of what he is in Christ. It is this unspeakable joy which makes you triumphant over the petty trials of life, and a victor over the testings that may come.

John said the purpose of our fellowship life was that we might have fullness of joy (I Jn. 1:3-4). Joy cannot be full without full fellowship. It is this joy of Christianity that makes Christianity the most attractive thing in the world. When joy goes, the Word loses its power, its freshness and richness. It is only when fellowship is at flood tide, and your heart filled with joy, that God is honored and souls are saved.

Fellowship in its fullness is the joy life with the throttle wide open on a down grade.

Yes, this joy of the Lord is one of the greatest things that comes to us in the new birth. It makes trouble lose its grip upon us; makes poverty lose its terror.

Remember : Jesus said, "My joy I give unto you." Jn. 15:11.

Again we consider the difference between joy and happiness. Both are to be desired; but it is far more important that we have joy than merely earthly happiness. Happiness depends on the things that we have or own; like property or loved ones. But joy is a thing of the spirit. It is an artesian well in the spirit that bubbles up, and overflows. It is the thing that comes as a result of the Spirit's working in our lives.

We read that the martyrs had joy unspeakable even when dying in physical agony ... that stirred the multitudes that thronged about, and startled men: How could they be so full of joy when they knew that death was near?

I've witnessed many Christians, going through deep sorrow, but have been kept by this unquenchable joy.

In years of evangelism, I've observed that joy is the real secret of evangelism. In our meetings, I've noticed that it is the joyful, living testimony that stirs the people. It is the person who is so full of joy that he can hardly speak, as the tears stream down his face, that moves the people. Yes, it is indeed the joyful testimony that touches hearts.

When we speak the Word with assurance and joy, it brings conviction to the listeners. When the Word becomes more real to you than any word man has ever spoken, you lips will be filled with laughter, your heart will be filled with joy, and you will have a victorious Christian life.

How many times I have seen that the hesitant testimony is a forerunner of failure, and the joyful testimony is a forerunner of victory.

Christians are only as strong as they are filled with joy of the Lord. A church is only as strong and influential for Christ in a community as it is filled with real joy of the Lord.

Why? "The joy of the Lord is your strength." Neh. 8:10. When people complain of lacking strength, or talk about how weak they are, often their real lack is the joy of the Lord.

When the Israelites return from Babylon to rebuild the walls of Jerusalem, Nehemiah found many of them were mourning and weeping; some were suffering with diseases; others were weak and undernourished. Not a few were downcast, defeated and despondent. But Nehemiah asked God for help for his people, and God gave them the message through their leader: "This day is holy unto the Lord your God; mourn not, nor weep. For all the people wept .... Neither be ye sorry; for the joy of the Lord is your strength." Neh. 8:9-10.

"The joy of the Lord is your strength!" This was God's answer for Israel then; it is God's answer for us today.

The joy of the Lord is not just a side-product the Lord gives to us. It is in actuality THE JOY OF THE LORD. It is not a selfish attribute to want to be full of the joy of the Lord. Christ Himself "who for the joy that was set before Him, endured the cross, despising the shame, and is set down at the right hand of the throne of God." Heb 12:2.

This joy of the Lord is our strength, and is a vital characteristic in receiving and maintaining good health. This joy is not only our strength spiritually, but likewise it ministers physical and mental strength to us.

GLADNESS vs. GLOOM

"This is the day which the Lord hath made; we will rejoice and be glad in it" Ps. 118:24.

20

The Lord makes for us each new day. Whatever God makes is good, and good for us. "And God saw everything He had made, and behold it was very good" Gen. 1:31. Since the Lord made the day, it's a day for good-living, not ill-living.

God made the day; He expects us to rejoice and be glad. "Serve the Lord with gladness" not sadness, commands Ps. 100. Say these words, "The Lord made this day for me: I shall be glad and rejoice!"

With God for me, with me, and within me, there's absolutely no room for gloom! God isn't a gloomy God, and He doesn't want gloomy children!

The Bible commands us, "Give no place to the devil." Eph. 4. When you give place for gloom in your life, you are giving place to the devil. He is the author of gloom.

Make it your glad declaration: in my life there's no room for gloom! Hallelujah!

So many of God's children are in low spirits. They are depressed, mopish, disgusted with life. Alright here is the positive way to lift yourself out of the doldrums: Make no more room for gloom, by being glad and rejoicing in the Lord ... always!

Right now walk out of your slough of despondency. Put a sudden stop to sulking! Life has much to dampen the spirit. But you are living by God's Word! Do not sink to the level of the pessimistic crowd. Quit wearing that long face. Your Lord is alive! He is risen! Shout hallelujahs!

Be a sparkling person, with no room for pouting, fretting and a dreary existence. Praise the Lord often. Count your blessings at bedtime, and it will surprise you what all the Lord has done!

Tune your ear with me now to a personal message from our God: "Fear thou not, for I am with thee; be not dismayed, for I am thy God; I will help thee; yea, I will strengthen thee; yea, I will uphold thee with the right hand of my righteousness" Isa. 41:10. How can you be down when God is holding you up? No more room for joyless, dismal living ... He is our God!

Congratulations, conqueror! There's no more room for gloom!

FREE FROM LONELINESS

It was during the last year of my high school. One Saturday evening, the news broke over the radio that our town was experiencing a "flash flood." Torrential waters were sweeping down from the canyon above our town and Manitou Creek was overflowing its banks.

Rapidly the streets flooded with water. An air of excitement was evident as the townspeople were out observing this sudden freak of nature.

Among those wading the knee-deep waters were my friend, George, and I. We were right across from the post office when we met one of our high school friends. Bonnie Bjorklun, and her mother. We paused a moment there on the sidewalk and talked about the "fun" the flood was.

We had hardly turned to go our way when we heard a blood-curdling scream. Quickly we looked back. It was Mrs. Bjorklun screaming as she gazed down at the sidewalk.

We rushed to her side. Immediately she pointed down an open manhole there on the sidewalk. With high-pitched wails, she explained that Bonnie had stepped into that manhole and was gone!

We were stunned to realize that only seconds before, we were standing within inches of that manhole that had been forced open by the raging flood waters. Yet in the darkness, it was not visible to us.

George and I accompanied Mrs. Bjorklun to her home where we were joined by her son, Dale, another classmate at high school. Personally I was overwhelmed by the awareness of how close I was at age 17 - to stepping into that manhole. Even though I held a Red Cross Life-Savers Certificate, my ability to swim strongly would not have helped in that enclosed drainage system with billowing flood waters!

When I returned to my room about 1 a.m., I dropped to my knees for a long prayer session with the Lord. Even though I accepted Christ as my Saviour at age 12, I had hardly allowed Him to be Lord of my life.

I felt so utterly alone that night. My parents had moved 1,500 miles away; I had spent most of that last year of high school living alone.

That loneliness persisted in the days ahead. I was a pallbearer at Bonnie's funeral. I was meeting God in prayer and study of His Word at every opportunity, primarily seeking His help to overcome my feeling of desperate loneliness.

In my Bible study, I discovered a scripture that was to change my life as only God's Word can do. It was Hebrews 13:5-6:

"For He hath said, I will never leave thee nor forsake thee; so that we may boldly say, The Lord is my helper, and I shall not fear what man can do unto me."

What an answer to my loneliness! No audible voice, nor bright lights. Just His pure Word that gave assurance.

Again on bended knee, I mediated on these facts: "Jesus Christ would be with me always, whatever the circumstance, good or bad. He would never leave me nor forsake me. I could count on His presence wherever I went. His sweet presence and peace would always minister to my natural loneliness."

HOW YOU CAN COUNT ON HIS PRESENCE

* In His last great Words to His followers, Jesus promised, "Lo, I am with you always, even unto the end of the world" Matthew 28:20. This is not a careless promise from the lips of the Master of all creation. He will be with us always.

* I encourage you to pray this prayer: "My dear Father, I thank you that you will be with me always, even as you have promised in your Word. I really need you, Lord; without you my life is so incomplete. I give you thanks that I need never be lonely because you will be with me always; you will never, never, never leave me nor forsake me. Thank you, Lord. Amen."

LIFTING POWER

God is very pleased with our praises. God says, "Whoso offereth praise glorifieth me" Ps. 50:23. God always manifests Himself in response to our praises (Ps. 22:3).

A defeated Christian is one who does not praise the Lord. A church with a defeated spirit has no joyful praise unto God. Praise and defeat cannot live in the same house!

Absolutely ... words of praise will lift you from defeat to victory, from sickness to health, from despair to joy, from bondage to liberty. Praise is the Language of faith, the Language of victory, and the Language of heaven.

To practice a positive praise life requires will-power and boldness, for the natural man doesn't like to praise the Lord. It's a wonderful spiritual exercise. The farther you are from God, the less you desire to praise Him. Worldly, carnal Christians do not enjoy the power and blessing of a positive praise life. Neither do people bound by fear, timidity or reluctance.

26

Lack of praise and thanksgiving is a spirit of these last days. "In the last days men shall become .... unthankful" 2 Ti. 3:2. God commands us to be full of thanks and praise. "Be ye thankful" Co.3:15. "Be thankful unto Him and bless His Name" Ps.100:4.

BEHOLD, unceasing praise ushers in the fulness of the Spirit. The 120 at Pentecost were "continually praising and blessing God" Lk. 24:53. Continual praise is a definite evidence of the Spirit-filled life (Eph 5:18-20).

Discipline your lips to praise the Lord. You will possess tremendous power, enjoy good health and keep Heaven "busy" working in your behalf. "By (Jesus) therefore let us offer the sacrifice to praise to God continually" He. 13:15.

HOW TO SPELL JOY

J JESUS FIRST **O** OTHERS NEXT **Y** YOURSELF LAST

JESUS First. Only "in the presence of the Lord there is fulness of joy" Ps. 16:11. Not in money, pleasure nor popularity, but in Christ. This joy is so vital for "the joy of the Lord is your strength" Neh. 8:10. This joy produces spiritual , physical and mental strength. "Though now we see HIM not, yet believing, we rejoice with joy unspeakable and full of glory" I

Pt. 1:8. "My joy," declared Jesus, "shall be in you, and your joy be full" Jn. 15:11. Jesus and Joy are synonymous.

OTHERS Next.

OTHERS

Lord, help me to live from day to day
In such a self-forgetful way,
That even when I kneel to pray
My prayer shall be for others.
Others, Lord, yes others,
Let this my motto be,
Help me to live for others
That I may live like Thee.

The joy of praying for others. "Ask and ye shall receive, and your joy shall be full" Jn. 16:24. We pray with joy: "Always in every prayer of mine for you all making request with joy" Ph. 1:4. Mighty answers come when we learn to pray for others. The result will be His wondrous joy!

The joy of witnessing to others. As a Christian our number one business is to be His witness (Ac. 1:8, Jn. 15:16). In the book of Acts, they were "joy-spreaders" when they were faithful in witnessing ... GREAT JOY came to Samaria through the bold witnessing of Philip, and again to the eunuch "rejoicing" was brought (Ac.

28

8:8,39). After witnessing for Christ in Ac. 13, we read these words, "The disciples were filled with joy." To discover this formula for joyful witnessing, read Ps. 126:5-6. Rom. 13:14.

The joy of fellowship. "That ye also may have fellowship with us, and truly our fellowship is with the Father, and with His Son Jesus Christ .... that your joy may be full" I Jn. 1:3-4. Fellowship is the true secret of joy. First, with the Father and Jesus (I Cor. 1:9). Then with others. Mal. 3:16-17, Heb. 10:25. Ac. 28:14-15.

YOURSELF Last. If you have lost joy, read Ps. 51:10-13, and make it your prayer. God's Word is the great joy producer (Jer. 15:16).

LOOKING LIKE A CHRISTIAN

"A merry heart maketh a cheerful countenance" Prov. 15:13.

Believe in the "doctrine of smiling." There are times to weep, to be in sorrow. But that is the exception, not the rule of the Christian life. Learn to say it often, " A smile is my style!" A smile is always in style.

Smile because you are a Christian. "REJOICE," said our Master, "Because your names are written down in heaven" Lk. 10:20. Cease lamenting. Quit murmuring and grumbling. You are God's child. God is for you, and who can be against you?

You should smile because it is less strenuous on your system than frowning or scowling. "Rejoice evermore. Sing with melody in your heart!" These are Bible commands.

A smile should be your style, when you know your rights in Christ. Speak it out loud, "I am more than a conqueror through Christ!" Rom. 8:37. Then look the part! When you know you are more than a conqueror through Christ, that God always causes you to triumph, it takes the unnecessary pressure out of life. You are no longer straining. The old whine is gone out of your voice!

A smile should be your style, because it makes you actually look better. And it improves your relations with others. To have peace of mind, a good nervous system and excellent health, you just must maintain wholesome relations with others. A real, genuine smile enhances your relations with others tremendously!

"The Lord hath made me to laugh," testified Sarah. The expression of holy laughter is a step beyond a smile. The Lord produces both within us. Laugh often!

A smile is the style of the triumphant in Christ! I dare you to live by this "power poem." It will improve your efficiency at least 33%

Enjoy God's best. Say it often: A SMILE IS MY STYLE!

"PROPHET, WRITER OR FRIEND?"

He was mockingly called 'the prophet.' Others ridiculed him as 'Santa Claus.' When he walked down a city street, people stopped and openly stared.

Mr. William Michaels was distinguished from others by an extraordinary, long white beard that flowed down to his waist. He stood out in any crowd and that's where I first saw him .... in the packed-out Chicago Coliseum where I was preaching the Gospel.

In his mid-seventies when we became friends, Mr. Michaels often traveled many miles by bus from his home in Wisconsin to attend the evangelistic crusades where I preached. On the opening night of each crusade, I would scan the audience for that familiar face and beard. Usually, Mr. Michaels would be there smiling and waiting to catch my eye.

As he listened to my messages, he would gently nod his head in approval. Afterwards, he would patiently stand near the platform, ready to give me words of encouragement or admonition. Mr. Michaels' godly influence affected me deeply.

At least twice a week, he would mail me lengthy easy-to-read letters - each page exuded with gems of spiritual wisdom. When an envelope bearing his unique hand-writing arrived in my post box, I would eagerly rip it open to devour his loving words of wisdom and guidance. Invariably, they were exactly what I needed for that particular moment.

He always treated me as a son. In one touching letter, Mr. Michaels wrote, "Don, I always yearned for one of my sons to become a minister, but none of them did. So I consider you 'my adopted son in the Gospel.' I am proud of you, Don," he continued, "and I pray fervently that God will use and bless your life."

God used this wonderful gentleman to motivate and guide me. Year after year his beautiful letters continued to inspire and enrich our fellowship.

One Christmas, his daughter-in-law conveyed the shocking news that Mr. Michaels had been called home to heaven. I was filled with grief over the loss of my precious, esteemed friend who had been such a vital part of my life for some years.

William Michaels had been a spiritual father. I Corinthians 4:15 says, "For though ye have ten thousand instructors in Christ, yet have ye not many fathers."

His anointed letters were constant source of guidance, comfort and encouragement. Now, his pen was forever silenced!

He had always prayed for my success in soul-winning. As he witnessed the crusades where God used me to win hundreds to Christ, tears of joy would spill from his eyes and stream down that long, white beard. Never again would I see his distinctive face in our crusade audiences!

Through the years, sweet memories of my friendship with this godly, sincere man have remained with me. Some people considered him to be an oddity because of his unconventional beard and appearance.

But to me, William Michaels was a man God sent to impart much practical wisdom to my young life. And he was my cherished friend.

"A wise man will hear, and will increase learning; and a man of understanding shall attain unto wise counsels" Proverbs 1:5.

HOW TO TREASURE FRIENDSHIPS

1. Realise God intentionally planned for you to have friends. Some relationships are especially significant. Sensitively, prayerfully evaluate each friendship to receive all God has to impart to you through it.

2. Loving, enduring friendship is a two-way street. Learn to give as well as receive. Adopt this motto: I live to give.

3. Cultivate communication that will enrich friendships. Words both written and spoken - are essential to healthy friendships.

4. Reach out in loving concern to minister to hurting friends. Remember: if nobody reaches, nobody gets touched.

DELIVERANCE FROM DESPONDENCY

"In the world ye shall have tribulation; but be of good cheer; I have overcome the world" John 16:33.

Often Jesus said to His disciples, "Be of good cheer." His very presence brought good cheer to their hearts. Jesus is good cheer personified! His Word is a message of good cheer.

Whenever a member of the Gossett family is downcast, we often challenge that one, "Be of good cheer."

"Good cheer" in the original Greek means, "Exercise courage, be bold, be confident, have confidence." To be of good cheer is real Bold Living.

In view of these facts, you should be filled with courage, very confident in Christ, bold as a lion and strong in faith.

Like Paul you should say to those around you that are fearful, apologetic and defeated: "Be of good cheer: for I believe God, that it shall be even as it was told me" Acts 27:25. Paul was on ship with hundreds of disheartened men. They were weary. They were brooding and melancholic, for their ship was in midst of a violent storm at sea.

"All hope that we should be saved was taken away," writes Luke the physician here in Acts 27. But like a giant stands Paul on this ship, and boldly affirms, "Be of good cheer, for there shall be no loss of any man's life!"

Why could Paul be so positive, so confident in the midst of certain disaster? Because of God's Word to him! That's why we can radiate this positive, unmistakable assurance in this day of turmoil: because of God's Word.

Because "God hath said .... WE MAY BOLDLY SAY" Heb 13:5-6. All because God has said it, we may now boldly say the same thing!

God's Word is irrefutable. It's clear, solid and reliable.

This is why we can be so sure, and declare, "Be of good cheer," for we have God's Word just as Paul did.

No more hesitation or wandering aimlessly, when we know the Word and the Author of it. To speak God's Word, and act upon it, isn't a leap in the dark. We are no longer unsettled, or indecisive. In every storm of life, we bring good cheer to our hearts, and to others, by boldly affirming, "Be of good cheer; it shall be even as God hath said!"

Every day affirm it: Good cheer is now here. Good cheer is Jesus. It is His Word.

Talking Life A Christian

"Whoso offereth praise glorifieth me: and to him that ordereth his conversation aright will I shew the salvation of God" Psalm 50:23

Words of praise glorify the Lord! I shall be a bold Praiser: one who praises the Lord. My resolve: "I will bless the Lord at all time; His praise shall continually be in my mouth" Ps. 34:1. As a Praiser, I extol the Lord, not so much for His gifts I receive, but I magnify the wonderful Giver Himself!

Words spoken in harmony with God's Word work wonders, too. I shall order my conversation aright. No "corrupt words shall proceed out of my mouth, but that which is good, to the use of edifying that it may minister grace to the hearers" Eph. 4:29.

Words of confession of God's Word indeed work wonders. My confession always precedes my possession. The word "confession" means to say the same thing. I dare to say exactly what God says in His Word. I agree with God by speaking His Word in all circumstances.

How Can I?

Talk sickness when the Bible says, "With His stripes we are healed" Isa. 53:5.

Talk weakness when the Bible says, "The Lord is the strength of my life" Ps. 27:1.

Talk defeat when the Bible says, "We are more than conquerors through Christ" Rom. 8:37.

Talk lack when the Bible says, "My God shall supply all my need" Phil. 4:19.

Talk bondage when the Bible says, "The Son has made me free" Jn. 8:36.

When I order my words aright, God manifests to me the benefits of His great salvation. "With the mouth confession is made unto salvation" Rom. 10:10. With my mouth I make confession unto salvation, which includes healing, deliverance and every spiritual and physical blessing provided for us in Christ. By words I overcome Satan (Rev. 12:11).

I know also that words can work blunders. Most of our troubles are tongue troubles (Pr. 21:21). A negative confession precedes possession of wrong things (Pr. 6:2). With the mouth confession can be made unto sickness, defeat, bondage, weakness, lack and failure. I refuse to have a bad confession.

My words work wonders. Words of praise. Words confessing God's Word. Words of bold authority expelling Satanic power. Words of singing. Yes, words are the "coin of the kingdom." I boldly speak words that work wonders!

SPEAK SUCCESS .... NOT FAILURE

Speak a new creation .... not the old creation filled with envy and rottenness. Declare it. "I am a new creature in Christ Jesus; the old things are passed away; behold all things are become new" II Corinthians 5:17.

Speak your righteousness in Christ .... not unworthiness. Affirm it, "I am the righteousness of God in Christ Jesus" II Corinthians 5:17.

Speak the language of the new kingdom of God's dear Son in which you now dwell .... not the old kingdom of darkness from which you have been translated. "Giving thanks unto the Father, which hath made us meet to be partakers of the inheritance of the saints in light; Who hath delivered us from the power of darkness, and hath translated us into the kingdom of His dear Son: in Whom we have redemption through His blood, even the forgiveness of sins" Colossians 1:12-14.

Speak that you are an heir of God and a joint heir with Jesus Christ .... not your old identification as a captive to sin and Satan. Testify to it. "I have a rich inheritance. I am blessed with every spiritual blessing. The Father Himself loveth me."

Speak that you have the life of God in your mortal

body ... not the old spirit of inferiority, failure and frustration. "In Christ you live and move and have your being" Acts 17:28.

Speak healing and health .... not how sick and diseased you are. Isaiah 33:24 foretells a future time when "the inhabitants shall not say, I am sick." That's a good practice in kingdom living now. Don't say. "I am sick," but speak the Word that heals. "With His stripes I am healed."

Speak financial success, not poverty and misery. Speak marriage success, not marriage failure. "Then thou shalt make thy way prosperous, and then thou shalt have good success" Joshua 1:8.

GLADNESS IN HIGH DEGREE

"Rejoice in the Lord always: and again I say, Rejoice" Ph. 4:4. Webster's dictionary defines rejoice: "To experience joy and gladness in high degree." The true object of our rejoicing is in the Lord Himself!

"Rejoice evermore" I Th. 5:16. This bold New Testament command is a two-word verse, but a high challenge. Above all others, we Christians must be a rejoicing people! Those who connect gloom and godliness misrepresent the Christian faith.

"I will rejoice in they salvation" Ps. 9:14. When we consider the great salvation we have by grace, it is indeed the call to a high degree of joy and gladness. Salvation! What a word! "Rejoice because your names are written down in heaven" Lk. 10:20.

"Rejoice ye in that day, and leap for joy: for behold, your reward is great in heaven" Lk. 6:23. In what day is Christ speaking of? In the day when men shall hate you, separate you from their company and reproach you. In this rejoice, be not sad!

"Jesus Christ, Whom having not seen, ye love; in Whom, though now ye see Him not, yet believing, ye rejoice with joy unspeakable and full of glory" I Pt. 1:8. Believing in Jesus is the key to always rejoicing!

Rejoicing is jubilant gladness. It may manifest itself in joyous laughter. The true Spirit-filled life will often result in such experiences as transpired on the Day of Pentecost, when the exuberant disciples were accused of being drunk on wine early in the day. Rather, it was an intoxication of the Spirit that had amazing results. So we today have the same fountain of joy open to us, in being Spirit-filled!

"Finally, my brethren, rejoice in the Lord" Ph. 3:1. And here are some of David's expressions: "Shout for joy," "Clap your hands," "Praise Him with a dance,"

"Exalt His Name," "Sing praises," "O magnify the Lord." Confess this now, "I will rejoice in the Lord always. This high degree of joy and gladness is a true antidote to the boredom of life, a stimulus that elevates the soul, that awakes the imagination and nerves the will to feats hitherto thought impossible." Filled with the Spirit of Christ, we are then beside ourselves .... in Him!

A SONG IN THE HEART

"Let the saints be joyful ... Let them sing aloud upon their beds. Let the high praises of God be in their mouth, and a two-edged sword in their hand." Psalm 149:5,6.

This is real Bold Bible Living .... to cultivate the singing heart!

The world has perverted song to purposes of evil passion. Such songs become one of the most alluring agencies of temptation.

But when we are converted, the Lord does some wonderful things for us. "He brought me up also out of a horrible pit, out of the miry clay, and set my feet upon a rock, and established my goings. And He hath put a new song in my mouth, even praise unto our God; many shall see it, and fear, and shall trust in the Lord."

Psalm 40:2,3.

When troubles come, learn to go at them with song! When griefs arise, sing them down! Praise God by singing; that will lift you above trials of every sort.

There are two primary secrets to maintaining a singing heart: (1) Be full of the Word; (2) Be full of the Spirit.

"Let the Word of Christ dwell in you richly in all wisdom; teaching and admonishing one another in psalms and hymns and spiritual songs, singing with grace in your hearts to the Lord." Col. 3:16.

When you are full of the Word, it produces a glad song. Confessing the Word aloud will bring forth an anthem of praise.

Hold Your Heart Steady With Song
I remember a time when I faced a most severe testing, that seemed would crush my spirit and bring me to frustrating defeat. The need was financial. I boldly began to affirm "My God shall supply all of my need according to His riches in glory by Christ Jesus." I kept it up for about 15 minutes, confessing it aloud over and over. In time that became a real song in my heart and mouth!

I resisted the temptation to doubt by singing praises unto God! As I held my heart steady by singing, the Lord worked miraculously in our behalf, and supplied the need!

Being full of the Word will cause you to "sing with grace in your heart to the Lord."

Then being filled with the Spirit will produce the same result. Eph. 5:18-20, "And be not drunk with wine, wherein is excess; but be filled with the Spirit; speaking to yourselves in psalms and hymns and spiritual songs, singing and making melody in your heart to the Lord; giving thanks always for all things unto God and the Father in the Name of our Lord Jesus Christ."

The Spirit-filled life, lived in the radiance of the Spirit, is wonderful! "I will sing with the Spirit, and I will sing with the understanding also" I Cor. 14:15. When you are controlled by the Spirit, He invariably inspires much song from your heart.

Every great move of the Spirit of past history was characterized by glad, gallant singing. What did Israel do when God delivered them from Egypt with a mighty hand? "Then sang Moses and the children of Israel this song unto the Lord .... The Lord is my strength and song, and He is become my salvation ....

I will exalt Him" Exodus 15:1,2.

What produced the most unusual intervention of God in sacred history? "And at midnight Paul and Silas prayed and sang praises unto God. And suddenly there was a great earthquake, so that the foundations of the prison were shaken: and immediately all the doors were opened, and everyone's bands were loosed" Acts 16:25-26.

Our circumstances may be dismal at times, and we may deplore the troubles besetting us. But our difficulties are usually mild compared to Paul and Silas. Their backs had been beaten to ribbons, they were thrust in that dirty, dark inner dungeon with their feet fast in the stocks.

But these men were "the righteous of the Lord bold as a lion" who could sing praises to God even under such circumstances. God intervened for them, and He will intervene for us, if we demonstrate such living confidence and bold faith in our God - to praise Him in song even when everything about us cries out, "Defeat!"

There is no defeat to the bold living Christian who knows this song, "Thanks be unto God who always causeth us to triumph through Christ" II Cor. 2:14.

"Serve the Lord with gladness; come before His presence with singing" Psalm 100:2.

"Sing aloud unto God our strength; make a joyful noise unto the God of Jacob" Psalm 81:1.

God delights in your song unto Him! Whether you have talent to sing or not, you are singing best when it is unto the Lord! Such song has wonderful power .... power to banish gloom, to quicken your spirit, to inspire you to bold courage!

In Heaven we shall be a singing people. Here on earth, we keep our hearts drawn heavenward by singing.

Fill your home with song. Teach your children to sing. Words in song are words that work wonders!

A PERSONAL SAVIOUR

Jesus Christ wants to be a wonderful personal Saviour to you. "Rejoice in the Lord always, and again I say, rejoice" Ph. 4:4. Not only a Saviour from sin and hell, but a Saviour from sickness, fear, worry and nervous disorder.

A lady from Saskatchewan wrote, "On your broadcasts you say that no Christian should ever suffer a nervous breakdown. But I have so many problems.

My husband is ill. My son is in the army overseas. My job is quite uncertain. How can I keep from being filled with worry and suffering with my nerves?"

My reply to this lady, "You have many reasons to worry, for your problems are great. And you are entitled to worry, unless you believe the Bible and in Jesus Christ as your personal Saviour. But if you believe in Christ and the Bible, as you can see, worry certainly isn't helping you. Worry never solved a problem, healed a sickness, nor paid a bill.

"I don't condemn you because you worry. But here is some positive advice: Christ your personal Saviour loves you and cares for you. He knows your problems, and promises to take your cares.

'Cast all your cares upon Him who careth for you' I Pt. 5:7. Let Jesus take each worry. Cast your burden upon the Lord. Then practice praising God. Real praise is the evidence of your faith. Rejoice in Christ your choice!"

Life is very real, filled with problems of all varieties. Observing God's order will heal your nervous disorder. Step by step take your cares and burdens right to the Lord. God really does care about the little things, as well as the big things. "Be careful for nothing, but in everything by prayer and supplication, with thanksgiving, let your requests be made known unto God. And the peace of God with passeth all understanding shall keep your hearts and minds through Christ Jesus our Lord" Ph. 4:7-8.

Affirm this joyfully, "I rejoice in Christ my choice. He's my personal Saviour from sin, sickness, fear, oppression, doubt and worry. Hallelujah, hallelujah, wonderful, wonderful Jesus!"

"As many as received Him to them gave He power to become the sons of God, even to them that believe in His Name" Jn 1:12. Receive Him by faith now, and He will be a personal Saviour to you.

THE LORD IS THE STRENGTH OF MY LIFE

The Lord is the strength of my mind, so today I think sound, healthy thoughts. I think upon those things that are true, honest, just, pure, lovely and of a good report. A strong mind is a positive mind, the mind of Christ. " I have the mind of Christ" I Corinthians 2:16.

The Lord is the strength of my ears, so I hear well today. Seven times in Revelation 2 and 3 the command comes, "He that hath an ear, let him hear what the Spirit saith ...." Most important, with my renewed, sound, strong mind, I hear what the Spirit saith unto me.

The Lord is the strength of my eyes, so I have good vision for today. I see others through eyes of love, kindness, and good will.

The Lord is the strength of my mouth, so I speak those words that are edifying, ministering grace to those who hear me. Isaiah 50:4, "The Lord God hath given me the tongue of the learned, that I should know how to speak a word in season to him that is weary: he wakeneth morning by morning, he wakeneth mine ear to hear as the learned." I refrain from speaking those words that are negative, destructive, corrupt, critical, harsh or unkind.

The Lord is the strength of my heart, so I have a good sound heartbeat for today. My prayer, "Lord, be thou the strength of my physical heart as long as I serve you on this earth. Yea, 70 years and by reason of strength 80 years or more." Oh heart, do your good work for this day.

The Lord is the strength of my hands, so that whatsoever my hands find to do, they do it with all their might.

The Lord is the strength of every organ, tissue, bone, fiber, nerve and cell in my body. The Lord is the strength of my life from the top of my head to the soles of my feet.

The Lord is the strength of my Life - my whole life - spirit, soul and body. He infuses strength into the hidden man of the heart.

My affirmations for today: Daniel 11:32, "The people that know their God shall be strong and do exploits." Psalm 29:11, "The Lord will give strength unto His people; the Lord will bless His people with peace." Philippians 4:13, "I can do all things through Christ which strengtheneth me" (not weakeneth me)> Nehemiah 8:10, "The joy of the Lord is my strength." Deuteronomy 33:25, "As my days are, so shall my strength be." II Corinthians 12:10, "When I am weak, then am I strong."

I affirm it five times:

"The Lord is the strength of my life"
"The Lord is the strength of my life"
"The Lord is the strength of my life"
"The Lord is the strength of my life"
"The Lord is the strength of my life"

I think strength. I believe in the Lord's strength. I talk strength. Joel 3:10, "Let the weak say, I am strong." I confess I am strong. Often I say, "Strength, Strength, Strength," as I speak the Word to my Spirit. Praise the Lord.

I, _____ , affirm the Lord is the strength of my life.

JOY UNSPEAKABLE

"Let the saints be joyful in glory: let them sing aloud upon their beds. Let the high praises of God be in their mouth, and a two-edged sword in their hand ... this honour have all His saints. Praise ye the Lord" - Psalm 149.

Each Christian has in his mouth either: no praises, low praises, or high praises.

No praises are indication of disobedience, carnality, ingratitude. "Because that, when whey knew God, they glorified Him not as God, neither were thankful; but became vain in their imaginations, and their foolish heart was darkened" Rom. 1:21.

Low praises are evidence of either a low-level fellowship with God, or a lack of knowing how to allow the Spirit to flow through you. Low praises are usually the effort of the natural man to praise. Low praises are shallow, feeble, short and accomplish much less than high praises.

High praises are the Spirit's flowing from your innermost being. Jesus declared, "He that believeth on me, as the scripture hath said, out of his belly shall flow rivers of living waters" Jn 7:38.

High praises are evidence of a joy-filled life. "Make a joyful noise unto the Lord, all the earth: make a loud noise, and rejoice, and sing praise" Ps. 98:4. This joy of the Lord is your strength. High praises are strong praises.

High praises are spontaneous, constant, "in everything," "for all things," "continually," "at all times."

High praises are the Spirit's expressions through you in spiritual songs, supernatural flowings, utterances both in the understanding and in the languages of the Spirit.

"The sacrifice of praise" is often low praises that, like the gears of a car, shift into high praises as you enter the flow of the Spirit!

High praises are harmonious, often loud, always an evidence the "two-edged sword" is in your heart and hand.

What kind of praises are in your mouth?

A MESSENGER OF CHEER

How, as a young Baptist minister, I received the baptism:

I had read many books for and against receiving the baptism. My decision: I wanted what they received in the Book of Acts as recorded in Chapters 2, 10 and 19.

Many hours I spent on my knees in an altar of prayer, pleading with God for this enduement of power Jesus promised in Luke 24:49, "And, behold, I send the promise of my Father upon you: but tarry ye in the city of Jerusalem, until ye be endued with power from on high."

Months passed, and I was yet without this Bible experience. I was hindered by fear: fear that I would no longer be accepted as a Baptist minister. My roots were deep in this great church. I was saved, baptized in water and called to preach in my dear Baptist church. One night I was challenged: "John the Baptist was filled with the Holy Ghost. Why not be filled with the Spirit, then you can be Don the Baptist!"

Thanksgiving holidays came with three days off

from my Bible College. I resolved: "I will not be denied. I will receive now." Wholeheartedness is a quality greatly commended in the scripture (Je. 29:13, Mt. 11:12).

The truth broke through to my spirit that the baptism of the Holy Spirit is a gift. Ac. 2:38, "Ye shall receive the gift of the Holy Ghost."

How does one receive a gift? Certainly not by begging, pleading, crying nor delaying. Simply by taking it and saying, "Thank you."

My attention was drawn to the practice of the original 120 Christians who received. What were they doing? "They were continually praising and blessing God" Lk. 24:53. Their attention was not so much on the gift, but rather it was upon the Giver Whom they were extolling, praising and blessing.

On that Thanksgiving night, I had hardly begun to praise Him with a whole and hungry heart, until I, too, received what they did: I began to speak with other tongues as the Spirit gave me utterance! Hallelujah, what glory filled my soul! For days I walked in the ecstasy of this One who filled my whole being. Most important, I had a new empowering to win souls to Christ.

You, too, can receive this wonderful Spirit-baptism. How? Sense your need. Abandon your fears. Cultivate a spiritual hunger. Don't be denied. Praise the mighty Baptizer Himself, and you shall receive!

FAITH FOR FAMILY FINANCES
An Open Letter To Fathers & Family Providers

Dear Father:

As a father and the provider for your family, I know how your honest spirit responds to the challenging words of I Timothy 5:8, "But if any provide not for his own, and specially for those of his own house, he hath denied the faith, and is worse than an infidel."

For the first 11 years I was the provider for the Don Gossett family, I experienced continual financial hardships and difficulties. Becoming the proud and happy father of five children by the time I was 28 compounded my problems, of course, for there were unrelenting financial requirements. Inability to meet my commitments on time produced embarrassment often. Those unexpected expenditures labelled emergency drained my resources and kept my back up against the wall.

In October, 1961, we were living in the beautiful island city of Victoria, British Columbia. Our financial situation was so deplorable, however, that it was hardly a pleasant experience.

Then, something happened that month that changed our picture in financial matters. What did happen is that after 11 years of defeats and nearly despair, God has ministered to us and through us to meet every need for the last 30 years!

It was an all-night prayer meeting that changed things for us. Joyce and I poured out our hearts to God. Perhaps I shall never forget my wife's prayers that night. I had never heard anyone talk so frankly to our heavenly Father. It wasn't just a nagging, complaining series of utterances either. As we concluded that night of prayer, we were confident that our needs would always be met from that night onward. And they have been, praise God.

God gave me a "secret" of faith for family finances that has never failed. He gave me "My Never Again List," as the foundation for a total change in my life. Point number 2: "Never again will I confess lack, for 'My God shall supply all my need according to His riches in glory by Christ Jesus!' Philippians 4:19." The Lord revealed to me how I had limited Him in ministering to my needs, because I constantly talked about my lack of money, my unpaid bills, etc. God asked me from Amos 3:3, "Can two walk together except they be agreed?" I couldn't walk with God in financial supply if I disagreed with Him. How was I disagreeing with God? By disagreeing with His Word. This Word of God became my new testimony. I agreed with God; I disagreed with the devil who was keeping his oppressive hands on the finances. Never again have I been victimized by lack of money for my family.

There are principles I have learned that are God's Word. God honours hard, diligent work. Labour is usually God's way to meet needs. Often God has met my needs by my writings. Writing is hard work. Sitting up all night on a train to deliver a manuscript to a publisher is also tedious. But even more rewarding than the financial returns are the thousands of lives transformed by words I have written under the inspiring leadership of the Holy Spirit.

Not just work, but faith. Your faith is detectible by your words. II Corinthians 4:13, "We then also having the same spirit of faith, according as it is written: I believed, and therefore have I spoken; we also believe, and therefore do we speak." Faith is released or expressed by your mouth. Speak your faith. That is, speak the Word. Say often, "My God shall supply all my need." Those are seven words that will put you over, even as they have put me over financially. God absolutely watches over His Word to perform it.

There is no doubt about it: What you say is what

you get. Speak of your lack of money, of how hard things are going for you and you will get what you say. I urge you to confess often, "I have faith for finances for my family. Thank you, Father, for thy riches now." With your palms open, reach out to your Father and receive from Him.

With love,
Don Gossett

MORE THAN A CONQUEROR

"In all these things, we are more than conquerors through Christ who love us"
Romans 8:37.

I am more than a conqueror through Christ. Jesus' death and resurrection provided me with salvation and abundant life. Christ's resurrection power is flowing through my veins, infusing me with His strength and enabling me to overcome any obstacle Satan hurls at me. I stall tall, strengthened in my inner man and boldly declare it: **I am more than a conqueror through Christ!**

Philemon 6 promises that "my faith becomes effectual by acknowledging every good thing which is in me in Christ." This is a good thing in me: **I am more than a conqueror through Christ!**

Speaking this truth with steady persistence produces ready insistence for a life of triumph. As my ears hear my lips speak God's Word, my faith grows, for "faith comes by hearing and hearing by the Word of God" (Romans 10:17). With a new surge of faith and power, I say what God says about my life: **I am more than a conqueror through Christ!**

I refuse to entertain doubts which suggest that I am less than what God says I am. There is no guesswork about it. This is a positive fact: **I am more than a conqueror through Christ!**

When depression or gloom seek to invade my spirit, prompting me to say "But I really don't feel like a conqueror ..." I forget my feelings and focus on God's Word. This is my declaration of faith not feelings: **I am more than a conqueror through Christ!**

When I am tempted to retreat from the positive profession position for fear that people might laugh if they hear me speaking with such confidence, I remember that this is God's Word I am confessing. I refuse to be influenced by the doubting crowd. I close my ears to doubt and ridicule. Instead, I open my mouth to fearlessly say what God says about me: **I am more than a conqueror through Christ!**

I resist the undermining thought: "It doesn't work for you...." I know this is God's own Word I am speaking and here is what God says about His Word: "So shall my Word be that goeth forth out of my mouth, it shall not return unto me void; but it shall accomplish that I please, and it shall prosper in the thing whereto I have sent it" Isaiah 55:11. God's Word is prospering in me - making me **more than a conqueror through Christ!**

When Satan relentlessly whispers "You have failed again ...." I reject his voice of accusation. Instead, I respond with God's Word that says **I am more than a conqueror through Christ!**

I voice my choice to be more than a conqueror.... not a defeated victim. I consistently confess these faith-filled, confidence-building declaration:

- "Sin shall have no dominion over me" (Romans 6:23). **I am more than a conqueror over sin.**

- Since "the Lord heals all my diseases" (Psalm 103:3), **I am more than a conqueror over sickness.**

- I agree with David by saying "I will fear no evil for the Lord is with me" (Psalm 23:4). Fear has no part in my heart! **I am more than a conqueror over fear.**

- By declaring "greater is He that is within me than
  he that is in the world" (1 John 4:4), **I am more
  than a conqueror over Satan.**

With emphasis on the underlined words, I
proclaim:

I am more than a conqueror through Christ!
I **am** more than a conqueror through Christ!
I am **more than a conqueror** through Christ!
I am more than a conqueror **through Christ!**
I am more than a conqueror through Christ!

What I confess is what I possess!

I, _____ , confess that I
am more than a conqueror through Christ who loves
me. I posses supernatural ability from God to be more
than a conqueror.

I AM SOLD ON BEING BOLD

I want to tell you why I'm sold on being bold as
a Christian. "The righteous are bold as a lion" Pr. 28:1.
You and I are righteous through Christ, and God
expects the righteous to be bold as a lion!

I'm sold because Jesus was bold. "Lo, He speaketh
boldly" Jn. 7:26. To be bold means to be confident,

courageous, fearless and daring. Jesus was our example in all of these qualities.

I'm sold because boldness is indeed a Jesus-like quality. "When they saw the boldness of Peter and John .... they took knowledge of them that they had been with Jesus" Acts 4:13.

I'm sold because the desire for boldness was the passion of the early Christians. They were filled with the Holy Spirit, they had been entrusted to use the Name of Jesus, they had the Word of God. But when they all prayed, here was their request: "Lord, grant unto thy servants, that with ALL BOLDNESS we may speak they Word" Acts 4:29.

I'm sold because the Holy Ghost produces this holy boldness. Of the early Christians we read, "They were all filled with the Holy Ghost, and spoke the Word of God with boldness" Acts 4:31. There are three Bible sins against the Holy Spirit that Christians can commit: We can resist the Spirit, quench the Spirit or grieve the Spirit. If we do not, but rather yield to the Spirit, He will produce boldness in us.

I'm sold because of the power of Jesus' Name. Acts 9:27 and 29 tells how Paul spoke boldly in the Name of Jesus. When we know that God has given Jesus the name above all names (Ph. 2:9-11), and that

Jesus has entrusted to us the use of His mighty Name, we will be bold to speak in His name against sickness, demons, fears, lack, financial needs.

I'm sold because speaking the Word boldly produces signs and wonders in confirming the Word. Acts 14:3, "Long time therefore abode they speaking boldly in the Lord, Who gave testimony unto the Word of His grace, and granted signs and wonders to be done by their hands." Peter and John spoke boldly at the beautiful gate, and the lame man was miraculously healed! Philip was bold in going to wicked Samaria, and the Lord worked mightily through him in mighty miracles!

I'm sold because of the blessing of bold praying. "Let us come boldly unto the throne of grace" Heb. 4:16. Bold praying is not loud praying necessarily; it is praying with real confidence and assurance. Bold praying also is "big praying," or expecting great thing from God through prayer. Read Jer. 33:3, Mk. 11:24, Jn 16:23.

I'm sold on being bold in giving. II Cor. 9:6, "But this I say, He which soweth sparingly shall reap also sparingly, but he that soweth bountifully shall reap also bountifully." Bold giving is giving bountifully, liberally, cheerfully.

THE ALPHABET OF HEALING
(26 Miracle-Producing Healing Scriptures)

The definition of ALPHABET is "the letters, marks or signs of a language used or conceived as a means of communication through written or verbal expression."

In the same way, the ALPHABET OF HEALING becomes the marks or signs of the "language of faith," conceived in God's Word and communicated by His children through verbal expression or the positive confession of the Word.

Now, begin using the miracle-producing healing scripture from the ALPHABET OF HEALING .... start believing and confessing your way to supernatural healing and health in Jesus' Name!

A. "ATTEND to my words; incline thine ear to my savings. Let them not depart from thine eyes; keep them in the midst of thine heart. For they are life to those who find them, and health to all their flesh." Proverbs 4:20-22.

B. "BELOVED, I wish above all things that thou mayest prosper and be in health, even as thy soul prosper" 3 John 2.

C. "CREATE in me a clean heart, O God; and renew a right spirit within me" Psalm 51:10.

D. "DEAL bountifully with thy servant, that I may live, and keep thy Word" Psalm 119:17.

E. "EFFECTUAL fervent prayer of a righteous man availeth much" James 5:16.

F. "FORGET not all His benefits ... who healeth all thy diseases" Psalm 103:3.

G. "GOD anointed Jesus of Nazareth with the Holy Ghost and with power: Who went about doing good, healing all that were oppressed of the devil; for God was with Him" Acts 10:38.

H. "HIMSELF took our infirmities and bare our sicknesses" Matthew 8:17.

I. "I am the Lord that healeth thee" Exodus 15:26.

J. "JESUS Christ the same yesterday, and today, and forever" Hebrews 13:8.

K. "KNOW ye not that your body is the temple of the Holy Ghost which is in you, which ye have of God and ye are not your own? For ye are bought with a price: therefore glorify God in your body and in your spirit, which are God's" I Corinthians 6:19-20.

L. "LAY hands on the sick and they shall recover" Mark 16:18.

M. "MERRY heart doeth good like a medicine, but a broken spirit drieth up the bones" Proverbs 17:22.

N. "NAME through faith in His name hath made his man strong whom ye see and know : yea, the faith which is by Him hath given him this perfect soundness in the presence of you all" Acts 3:16.

O. "OUGHT not this woman, being a daughter of Abraham, whom Satan hath bound, lo, these eighteen years, be loosed from this bond?" Luke 13:16.

P. "POWER of the Lord was present to heal them" Luke 5:17.

Q. "QUICKEN your mortal bodies by His Spirit that dwelleth in you" Romans 8:11.

R. "RESIST the devil and he will flee from you" James 4:7.

S. "SENT His word and healed them" Psalm 107:20.

T. "TALK ye of all His wondrous works" Psalm 105:2.

U. "UNTO you that fear my Name shall the sun of righteousness arise with healing in His wings" Malachi 4:2.

V. "VIRTUE went out of Him and healed them all" Luke 6:19.

W. "WITH His stripes we are healed" Isaiah 53:5.

X. "EXPECTATION is from Him" Psalm 62:5.

Y. "YOUTH is renewed like the eagles" Psalm 103:5.

Z. "ZEALOUS of spiritual gifts" I Corinthians 14:12.

PLEASANT WORDS:
HEALTH TO THE BONES (Proverbs 16:24)

Pleasant words are word pleasing to God. Words pleasing to God are in harmony with His own Words and words that He directs us to speak.

God declares, "Whoso offereth praise glorifieth me" Psalm 50:23. Pleasant words - words pleasing to God are words of praise and words spoken in harmony with the Word. These pleasant words of praise produce health benefits. When praise becomes a way of life, God is glorified and manifests the benefits of His salvation. Salvation includes healing! Satan the oppressor (Acts 10:38) is the cause of our health problems and mental disturbances. But Satan is allergic to praise, so where there is massive, triumphant praise, Satan is paralyzed, bound and banished. Praise produces the atmosphere where God's presence resides (Psalm 22:3). Therefore, praise is the most effective shield against Satan and his attack. Praise is the signal to Satan of his defeat; it's the most devastating weapon we can use in our conflict with Him.

When David Wilkerson was in the early part of his work among the gangs of New York City, he encountered a group of boys on a street corner. As he approached them, there were signs that they were preparing to attack. Looking to the Lord for guidance, David continued to advance. At the instant they seemed poised to strike, David suddenly clapped his hands and shouted "Praise the Lord." The entire gang broke ranks and fled. The only plausible explanation for the action is that these boys were activated by evil spirits who panicked at the shout of praise. Pleasant words of praise spoken by David proved to be health to his bones literally!

"Pleasant words are as an honeycomb, sweet to the soul, and health to the bones" Proverbs 16:24. The reverse of this scripture would read: "Unpleasant words are bitterness, unforgiveness, malice; devastating to the soul; and will destroy your health and well-being."

Pleasant words are not just nice little dainties. Pleasant words are powerful because they harmonize with heaven, administer health benefits and are characterized by much praise!

HOW FORCIBLE ARE RIGHT WORDS
- Job 6:25

There is a great power in your mouth to speak right words that are forcible and dynamic in their working. Speak in the Name of Jesus. "Whatsoever ye do in word or deed, do all in the name of the Lord Jesus, giving thanks to God and the Father by Him" Colossians 3:17. It's not superstition nor mysticism to speak often His wonderful Name. "The Name of the Lord is a strong tower; the righteous runneth into it and is safe" Proverbs 18:10.

Jesus gave us the right to speak in His Name. The

"ask" of John 14:13-14 implies "commanding in the Name of Jesus" diseases, demons and adverse circumstances to depart! The "ask" of John 15:16 and 16:23-24 refers to praying to the Father in the all-powerful Name of Jesus. Jesus is the name above all names (Philippians 2:9-11). How forcible is His majestic Name! I challenge you to speak His Name often. Right now say "Jesus" three times!

In crusades in Nagercoil, Tamul Nadu, and Trivandrum, Kerala, India, I faced thousands of people each night in our open air crusades. Over and over I invoked the Name of Jesus in commanding the diseases to depart. In Nagercoil, 77 notable miracles were recorded. Similar results took place in Trivandrum. You, too, can receive healing through His Name. "And His Name through faith in His Name hath made this man strong, whom ye see and know: yea, the faith which is by Him hath given him this perfect soundness in the presence of you all" Acts 3:16.

In India I had the immense joy of leading tens of thousands of people to saving faith in Jesus Christ. As these multitudes believed in the death, burial, and the resurrection of Jesus Christ and confessed Him as Lord of their lives, they received Everlasting Life! You, too, can be saved now. "For the same Lord over all is rich unto all that call upon Him. For whosoever shall call upon the Name of the Lord shall be saved"

Romans 10:12-13.

Words of praise are forcible words. Praise is the spark-plug of faith, the one thing needed to get your faith airborne, enabling you to soar above deadly doubt. Speak words of praise often.

GEORGE Gallup in his international religious poll discovered that of all the peoples of the world, the people of India are "the most hungry for God."

Having invested a part of my life in this land of 900 million, and having ministered to their hungering hearts, I can affirm that of the 40 nations I have gone with the Gospel, the people of India are the hungriest people I've encountered!

In Nagercoil, Tamul Nadu, we stayed at the Cape Hotel, at the very bottom of India where the Indian Ocean, the Arabian Sea and the Bay of Bengal all converge into one body of water. Driving into the city twice daily for our crusade services, we would pass lovely rice paddies, towering mountains, rivers where people were bathing and washing clothes. But virtually lining every highway and street were people, precious people for whom Jesus died. In the crusades they came by the tens of thousands to receive Jesus Christ by believing in His resurrection and confessing Him as Lord of their lives.

My Tamul interpreter was Brother David, a pastor from Madras. My Malalam interpreter was Brother Samuel, a minister of the Assemblies of God. Both men had memorized great portions of scripture. Hence, I could quote whole verses at a time without stopping. These fine interpreters would translate my words intact. It was a joy to flow with these men in preaching the Gospel. They were anointed by the Holy Spirit as I was.

We were met at the Trivandrum airport by Mr. Chandry, an official of the government of India. He graciously welcomed us to his land. At the final breakfast before our departure, we met with the pastors and officials. Mr. Chandry spoke first. He shared how he had walked all over the grounds of the Police Stadium where the crusade was conducted. He estimated the closing night attendance to be 150,000 people!

I sincerely look forward to returning to India's masses again and again.

COLD FEET AND A YELLOW STREAK

"The fear of man bringeth a snare"
- Proverbs 29:25

Cold feet and a yellow streak is fear and a lack of

courage, bordering on cowardice. What are the symptoms? You would be used of God but you are afraid of people's opinions of you. You would speak up for Jesus but you are hemmed in by the fear of man. You would be bold in using the Name of Jesus; you withhold because you are afraid of failure, or that someone may criticize you. You would love to place your hands upon the sick for recovery, but you draw back because you are afraid you would be branded a "healer," or a fanatic. God warns, "Now the just shall live by faith; but if any man draw back, my soul shall have no pleasure in him." Hebrews 10:38.

As a child I had a bad case of cold feet and a yellow streak. The first day I entered school, I kept my head on my desk all day long, because I didn't want to look at others, or have others look at me. When visitors would come to our home, I would hide away in a closet or crawl under a bed, so I wouldn't have to meet strangers. What hangups! But how real they were! I have had a lifelong battle with a tendency to avoid eye contact with people, likely another symptom of this ailment .... cold feet and a yellow streak. When I was elected president of my high school student body, I fumbled with words as I led those student body assemblies that were agony to me. Also, I have had to wrestle with an overly sensitive man-pleasing attitude.

But God has helped me. I am debtor to help you

73

that are captives to cold feet and a yellow streak. I took the words God spoke to Moses. "Now therefore go and I will be with thy mouth and teach thee what thou shalt say" Exodus 4:12. God promised to be with my mouth, even as He was with Moses' mouth. I learned to speak freely, instead of faltering, hesitant speech.

Here are key prayers I've employed in overcoming cold feet and a yellow streak. Daily I make my earnest prayer, the same prayer God so mightily answered for the early Christians: Acts 4:29-30. "Lord, behold their threatenings, and grant unto thy servants that with all boldness they may speak thy Word, by stretching forth thine hand to heal, and that signs and wonders may be done by the Name of thy holy child Jesus." Another strong prayer, Ephesians 6:19-20, "Grant that utterance may be given unto me, that I may open my mouth boldly ... that I might speak boldly as I ought to speak." This has given me authority in God-given bold speech. What a contrast when governed by cold feet and a yellow streak and its characteristic negative, reluctant speech habits!

I challenge you: be done with cold feet and a yellow streak (fear and cowardice). Life is too short to be fettered by a fear of man's opinions. When God desires to flow through you in one of the gifts of the Holy Spirit or be used of Him in supernatural ministry to the oppressed, fearlessly step out to be used of Him.

74

When I have faced crowds of tens of thousands night after night in India in our crusades, how grateful I was that God had delivered me from cold feet and a yellow streak. The bolder my faith, the greater the victories in salvation of multitudes and the healing of the sick.

I charge you: be done with cold feet and yellow streak. God has not given you the spirit of fear, but of power, and of love, and of a sound mind (II Timothy 1:7). There's a verse against fear for every day of the year. Fortify yourself from these words: "For He hath said, I will never leave thee, nor forsake thee. So that we may boldly say, The Lord is my helper and I shall not fear what man can do unto me" Hebrews 13:5-6. Love the brotherhood. Honor all men. But never fear any man, nor what man can do unto you.

What you confess is what you possess. What you is what you get. Say it boldly. "God sets me free from every spirit of fear. I am no longer bound by man's opinions. I am free in Jesus. I will daringly do God's will for my life. I shall be bold in being used of God. With all confidence I shall minister in Jesus Name, no man forbidding me. Fear has no part in my heart!"

WHAT YOU SAY IS WHAT YOU GET!

Why do you get what you say? Jesus declared

emphatically, "Whosoever shall say unto this mountain, be thou removed, and be thou cast into the sea, and shall not doubt in his heart, but shall believe that those things which he saith shall come to pass, he shall have whatsoever he saith" (Mark 11:23). This is an awesome Bible promise. Before I explain how to get what you say, I want to get in one word of warning: since what you say is what you get, don't ever say anything you wouldn't want to get. "Whoso keepeth his mouth and his tongue, keepeth his soul from troubles" (Proverbs 21:23). And Jesus said, "That every idle word men shall speak, they shall give account thereof in the day of judgment. For by thy words thou shalt be justified, and by thy words thou shalt be condemned" (Matthew 12:36-37).

"Can two walk together except they be agreed?" (Amos 3:3). You can never walk with God in blessing, triumph and abundant supply as long as you disagree with God's Word. Here is the secret: you get what you say when you agree with God's Word. Say what God says about your life. Say what He says about your health, your finances, your strength, your anointing, your power, about all the blessings God has promised in His Word.

"That the communication of thy faith may become effectual, by the acknowledging of every good thing which is in you in Christ Jesus" (Philemon 6). Your faith becomes effectual; that is, you get good and great thing from God by acknowledging every good thing in you in Christ Jesus! Acknowledging is saying what God says, agreeing with the Word, affirming the promises. It is declaring who you are in Christ, what you have in Christ, what you can do in Christ.

"The Word is nigh thee, even in thy mouth and in thy heart; that is, the Word of faith which we preach" (Romans 10:8). How does the Word of faith function? It is the Word in your mouth and in your heart. When the heart and the mouth flow in harmony, faith is operative and faith is the victory!

- You say, "There is therefore no condemnation to me for I am in Christ Jesus" (Romans 8:1); you get freedom from condemnation.

- You say, "Where the Spirit of the Lord is, there is liberty" (II Corinthians 3:17); you get liberty in the Lord because your body is the dwelling place of the Holy Spirit.

- You say, "I am casting all my cares upon Him Who careth for me" (I Peter 5:7); you get a "carefree" life because all your cares are cast upon the Lord.

- You say, "By Whose stripes I am healed" (I Peter 2:24); you get healing from all your diseases.

- You say, "Christ Jesus is made unto me wisdom from God" (I Corinthians 1:30); you get wisdom to cope with all life's crises.

- You say, "God always causeth me to triumph in Christ" (II Corinthians 2:14); you get triumph in all things.

- You say, "Greater is He that is within me than he that is in the world" (I John 4:4); you get authority and dominion over the works of the devil.

- You say, "The Lord is the strength of my life" (Psalm 27:1); you get strength for your day.

- You say "God hath given to me the measure of faith" (Romans 12:3); you get all the faith you need to overcome in life.

- You say, "God hath not given me the spirit of fear, but of power, of love, and of a sound mind" (II Timothy 1:7); you get freedom from fear.

- You say, "My God shall supply all my need" (Philippians 4;19); you get the supply of every need.

- You say, "I can do all things through Christ Who strengtheneth me" (Philippians 4:13); you get Christ's ability to be an achiever in life.

FINAL WORDS

You have read, so now rejoice. Put into practice the new inspiration you have gained through your study of this message.

As the joy of the Lord is yours now, remember that joy is maintained and increased only as your praise the Lord, and by love serve others.

I shall be glad to hear from you. Tell me, please, what this message on glad Christianity has done for you.